Kiss Me

LIKE YOU MEAN IT

A Journey of Love and Passion

THOMAS THEOPHILUS

Quantum
Discovery
A LITERARY AGENCY

Library of Congress Control Number: 2025907142

ISBN
979-8-89641-063-8 (Paperback)
979-8-89641-064-5 (eBook)
979-8-89641-062-1 (Hardcover)

TO THE READER:

I feel everyone should write or at least keep a journal. I call it my "Self-Therapy," it is truly therapeutic to see your words, feelings, emotions reflecting back at you! So I hope you will at least give it a try you may surprise yourself!

TABLE OF CONTENTS

MOONBEAMS CAST

CLOUDS OF TIME

KISSED BY DESIRE

DISCLAMER:

The publisher and the author are providing in this book and its contents on an "as is" basis and make no representations or reflections of any kind with respect to this book or its contents. The publisher and the author disclaim all such representations and reflections, including but not limited to anything that could cause harm to another person of or for a particular purpose. In addition, the publisher and the author assume no responsibility for errors, inaccuracies, omissions, or any other inconsistencies herein.

The content of this book is for informational purposes only and is not intended to harm or misrepresent any person. You understand that this book is for the purpose of entertainment only! Please understand that all words belong to God, and we only rearrange them. Your reading of this book implies your acceptance of this disclaimer.

The publisher and the author take no responsibility concerning the level of heart felt words that effect people in many different ways. If any words comingle with those of others it is simply by coincidences.

Pictures were chosen at random for this book that others had shared already on the internet, and the publisher and the author lays no claim to any of them.

PROLOGUE

❧

The Lord is my shepherd I shall not want

He maketh me to lie down in green pastures: he leadeth me beside the still waters.
He restoreth my soul: he leadeth me in the paths of righteousness for his name's
sake. Yea, though I walk through the valley of the shadow of death, I will fear
no evil: for thou art with me; thy rod and thy staff they comfort me.

Thou preparest a table before me in the presence of mine enemies:
thou anointest my head with oil; my cup runneth over.

Surely goodness and mercy shall follow me all the days of my life:

and I will dwell in the house of the Lord forever.

Psalms 23

MOONBEAMS CAST

A FIRE I CAN'T PUT OUT

When there is nothing else to do,
And there is little left to pursue–
Then my thoughts turn to you,
And in my world I have a better view.

Things can change in a blink of an eye,
That is something I can never deny–
When love is good it's at its best,
That's why I treasure you above the rest.

The affect that you have upon me
Has caused me to achieve all you see–

Like each star that is set in heaven above,
They count for all the words you said in love.

Together there will never be a shredded tear,
And in my arms you are secure without fear–
You have brought meaning to a life worthwhile,
And I face every tomorrow with a smile.

To my heart is a perfect love that you've made,
But as time passes know it will never fade–
It's once in a life time that a dream comes true,
It's not about me, but it's always about you!

I could look into your eyes forever and a day,
And when sadness comes you take it all away–
So when this life is over this you should know:
"I loved you more than I could ever show."

© April 6, 2011

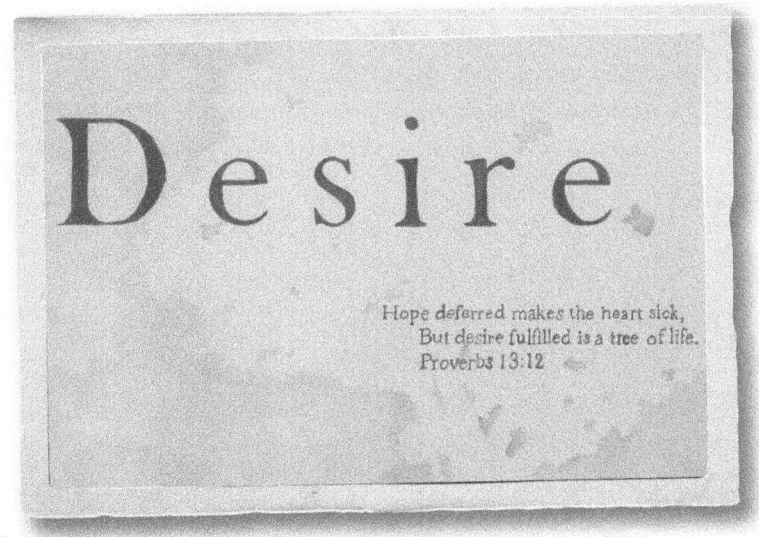

Hope deferred makes the heart sick,
But desire fulfilled is a tree of life.
Proverbs 13:12

BURNING WITH DESIRE

An old, old love, that set
my heart on fire
Upon her body I could feel the heat,
A passion that was beyond any desire,
As she left her love stains on the sheet.

O how passion dripped from her eyes
That set my inner soul aglow—
And in the night I can still hear her cries
A love that only this heart will ever know.

Why I let her slip away is still confusing—
Kisses so sweet – that truly blew my mind!
I stop and laugh, yes that was so amusing,
Then I take another sip of wine…

An old, old love, that set my heart on fire—
Yes darling, I'm still burning with desire!

© September 15, 2019

CHASING THE WIND

The wind blows to the south and turns to the north,

Round and round it goes, ever returning on its course.

The streams flow to the sea, yet the sea is never full.

To the place the streams come from, there they return again.

The eye never has enough of seeing, nor is the ear full of hearing;

Though we never stop chasing the wind.

We search for wisdom to teach us what the right path to take in life is,

The more learned we become the less we seem to know.

What is twisted cannot be straightened; what is lacking cannot be counted.

The pleasures we seek to sustain us are gone with the morning's light,

And we ask are we wise or a fool, but in the end fate overtakes them both;

Though we never stop chasing the wind.

The ladder of success is an endless climb to rise above all,

And to be recognized for all of our great accomplishments.

For man may do his work with wisdom, knowledge and skill,

And then he must leave all he owns to someone who has not worked for it.

In the midst of all the gathering and storing of wealth who did we thank?

Though we never stop chasing the wind.

It is not good to be alone on this journey we take through life,

For two are better than one, because they have a good return for their work,

And if one should fall down, then the other can help him up again.

Also, if two lie down together, they can keep each other warm,

But how can one weather the storms of life alone?

Though we never stop chasing the wind.

Whoever loves money never has money enough, and is always seeking more;

If a man loves wealth he is never satisfied with his income.

Cast your wealth upon the waters, for after many days you will find it again.

Give to the needy, yes the needy, for you do not know when you will need.

Sow your seed of love, and love you will reap for your good deeds;

Though we never stop chasing the wind.

Solomon with all his wisdom did not understand the path of the wind,

Or how a body is formed in a mother's womb, so we too cannot understand

The work of God, the maker of all things…

Live your days and be happy without anxiety, for God will judge all in the end,

And remember the dust returns to the ground, and your spirit returns to God;

Though these words you may not believe, but in time you also will stop…

"Chasing the wind."

HONEY FROM A THORN

The life we live we just watch as it goes,
With little thought of how sweetly it flows
As long as we have on our back pretty clothes,
But in our heart the truth always shows.

Then, we close our eyes so we can't see
That time and money didn't set us free,
And we blame others for what couldn't be,
But in the end it's up to you and me.

All we remember are the hurts and scorn,
Never giving credit for the
days that were warm,
At least we have the sweetness of a frosty morn,
For life can be like licking honey from a thorn.

© June 30, 2002

IN MY ARMS

The sweet salty tears I've cried
Hurts my heart has tried to hide,
And those times…
I have needed you in my arms,

Sounds of music upon the strings;
The times I griped the porcelain god,
The heaves, the one night flings–
Life hammered down like a steel rod!

Passion screaming within my heart,
Cigarettes burning in an ash tray;
Thinking God, I can't play this part,
Please make her memory go away!

Four o'clock and I'm afraid to crash
Ice crackles in an empty glass…
Love and passion are my crimes,
And I know in time this will pass.

The nights I've abused this life,
The sweet salty tears of my strife…
Wakening up in the strangest places,
Remembering time, but never faces!
Flashing lights – deafening alarms…
Needing you in my arms…

© April 23, 2015

7

IT'S ME AGAIN

Good Morning Lord! Yes it's me again,
And I know your words are true,
But Lord, I'm not sure what to do…
"Remember, if the mountains fall into the sea
I'm still in control – so please let it all be!"
Lord the world is in such a mess…
"My child," if you lean on Me you'll find rest!
Watch the clouds in the east – there I'll appear,
And with Me all the Saints will be near–

Gabriel's trumpet will make a mighty sound!
Then all believers will rise from the ground–
And the world will know it's the end!
Yes Lord, I know that will be a glorious day
I guess I just let the world get in my way!

© June 3, 2023

KILLING ME SOFTLY

Passion, why do you dingle me on a string,
And taut my spirit until early spring,
Awaken me when the autumn leaves shake
Even on the shallow waters of a lonely lake,
But to me the wind shall paint in the skies
Where this passion has reflected in her eyes,
But these sweet words are killing me softly—
And in the silence of night I hear her cries,
Where my soul hides and is not willing to see,
Because I'm afraid that it's nothing but lies.

In my thoughts I drift across the years,
I think of the times when I was low than high
On some stimulant to help my life go on by,
But now dear love I have no time for tears!
As I search for your spirit somewhere in the sky,
Hoping you will return upon the Eagles wings
Knowing its but a fleeting thought that stings—
If I could think of sweet words that would rhyme
To draw upon my soul that hides this secret thing-
That's killing me softly without committing a crime,
Then I know my spirit will have a reason to sing.

© December 31, 2004

9

GO WITH THE EBB

Your beauty is like the light,
Bright, like the essence of time.
Like the joy of a rose opening,
Pink is for the color of love,
Red is for your lips of passion,
Yellow is as the sunlight of day
That warms a soul of giving.
Blue is for your eyes that holds
Me in a trance of total desire.
Green is for the envy when others
Wish they were in my place.
The sound of your voice
Is like the receding of a tide
That whispers its own music.
I can hear the wind calling with
Each capping of a wave that
Lures the touching of our souls;
Two hearts melted together
As one until time is no more!
Will you sail life's sea with me?
And go with ebb's loving flow.

© May 10, 2011

DO YOU REMEMBER TOO?

The night was tender when I laid you down,
Those moments of love you and I found…
The music was playing so soft and low,
And the candles flicker under the moon's glow—
Your skin of velvet – your lips of honey, too,
O how I remember – do you?
It was as if we left the world behind…
Enchanting moments that forgot about time!
The troubles in life just passed us on by,
And our hearts never questioned why?
Memories made in a night's intimate world,
Love made to a beautiful girl—
Now I pen my thoughts for that's all I can do,
O how I remember – do you?

© August 2, 2017

CALIFORNIA GIRLS

We walked upon the sands at Santa Cruz,
As the Pacific sun was sinking low…
The waves were crashing against the shore,
And you mentioned that in your last letter–
I answered it, but I never heard from you!
I remember you making fun of my accent,
And my Southern Charm – you were so cute
With your dimples, and such a sweet smile!

I still think about you when I hear…
"Do you know the way to San Jose?"
We never know the course of life we'll take,
And one thing is certain – we can't go back!
I wish they all could be California girls…
But I've opened a lot of clams to find a pearl.

© June 5, 2001

HELLO WORLD

I look at all the madness today,
And I question what to say–
Everyone appears so angry,
And lost in their misery!
I have to look at my own sanity,
And the state of humanity–
What has happened to our morality?
The truth we can't seem to see-
We live in a world of greed,
And we forget what others need!
We are standing on shaky ground,
And this is what I have found:
"If you take God out of everything,
Then we are left with misery and pain."

© March 24, 2021

LILIES BY THE POND

Time…

Thoughts of regret…

Like lilies by the pond

Where a lonely heart still cries for you

The silence in my soul knows no rest

The sounds in the night seems to go on

The touches of your skin I remember

Our hearts entangled with endless love,

And now yesterday hangs in my mind

Like the wind that plays in the lilies…

© *December 17, 2016*

MOUNTAIN VIEW

I have walked for hours to reach this magnificent view
Atop this beautiful mountain I can see for endless miles
Just in time to see the sun rising in the eastern sky
The smell of Rhododendron is thick in the morning air,
And the fog has now begun to give way to a new day.

What I'm about to witness words will never give it justice
The peacefulness that God has laid before me–
The sounds of the stillness – so quiet I can hear my heart beat
I feel a gentle breeze that embraces my very existence–
It's like reaching out and regaining a spirit that was lost.

In the distance a Red Hawk is scoring high on the thermals

If I could only ride on his wings – this freedom I surly need

The maples are standing tall as a Wood Hen gives out a call–

A small lake reflects the mountains with their majestic beauty

The green Ponderosas are reaching to touch the sky of blue.

A gentle stream is flowing gracefully down the mountainside

If I had any troubles today – would you carry them far away?

The fawn stops to take a drink with her ears perched as to say:

"Yes, I know you are watching me, and I can feel your love,"

What have I done to deserve this moment, and then I think of you.

In the low lined meadows below the wild flowers are all in bloom

Daisies, golden rods, red poppies, and crimson clover fields, too

I'm so honored with such a view, as my tears dry, where are you?

Before me lies what's real in this life: "In God's most perfect view!"

For it is here within this beauty I give all my love to you!

© December 25th, 1999

THE BREAKING OF BREAD

The walls reflected years of a forgotten time
As the grapevines hanged above the street;
Corks being popped from old bottles of wine,
In Mustache's Bistro a' vines where people meet.
No candles on the wooden tables for us to burn,
And long ago the timbers were set in masonry;
The wisdom we gained and the words we learned,
Precious moments etched in time and in memory.
Here one could find what most have lost in life,
And to know in our hearts there was still room;
To face another tomorrow with a little less strife;
As shadows fell gracefully from an autumn moon.
We took time to break bread and let our hearts arise!
A time experienced in the joy of our lovers' eyes.

© September 15, 2004

17

PATH OF DESTINY

My Dad died when I was a small lad,
And thoughts of that still make me sad,
But in that short time I was taught so much,
And to that knowledge I still have to clutch!
His mentoring lost was an agony to my heart,
But in truth, my whole world just fell apart!
So all my life I've had this void of total loss,
And without his direction I've paid the cost!
I know in my heart it was not his fault–
But to flavor life one needs their Dad's salt!
Now I find I have fought so hard to save–
The wealth of love that he so graciously gave,
A reflection of him you can now see in me–
But circumstances set this: "path of destiny."

© *January 17, 2019*

18

SMOKE IN THE WIND

As I sit in silence waiting for the words to flow,
There is sadness, from whence I do not know.
The misguided paths of my life were only for a living,
Did I forget to live and take what I was given?

Why are my dreams and realities always at war?
Fears so deep within my heart, I cannot ignore!
Wisdom is something we gain only by living,
The courage not to take a chance can be unforgiving.

If we could only restore the broken spirit of our soul,
And uphold the essence of life and relinquish control.
Given the freedom of our choices in all we say and do,
One would think that we could find a better view.

Knowledge of life is more valuable than silver or gold,
The more learned we become the less we seem to know!
By wisdom alone our lives should always be built,
Just establish love and trust, and it will never wilt.

Listen my friends! Consider my words and lend an ear,
Although life is fragile and we hold it so very dear,
Let's live life to the fullest – even until death's very end!
For a moment in time it will be as "smoke in the wind."

© 1999

TOUCHES OF A WOMAN

Like the velvet pedals of a rose,
And in your heart you know–
A smell that lingers in my mind,
Because I love to touch you so.

The fragrance of your perfume,
In every move I take…
It fills the corridors of my being,
And your love I'll never forsake!

I carry you in my heart each day,
And I know the years have passed–
Mine eyes can't hold all the tears
Just to think, love cannot last.

Touches of a woman – your face,
Imagines of love set in every place.

© May 22, 2019

UPON THE GRASSY KNOLL

The evils of men were not from on high
But their plans were devious and sly.
As cameras flashed from frame to frame
Today he shall die they boldly proclaimed!
The horror that fell upon Dallas that day
Put a picture of men's hatred on display.
Sorrows were scattered across our land
With sadness we will never understand.

The shots rang out with an ominous sound
With rhetoric for truth that was never found.
Soon the tragedy of that day would prevail
As a stunned crowd graveled with their tale.
In this moment God was the only one to call
For the powers at hand had deceived us all.
Then there was mourning upon this earth
For the one ordained from his given birth.

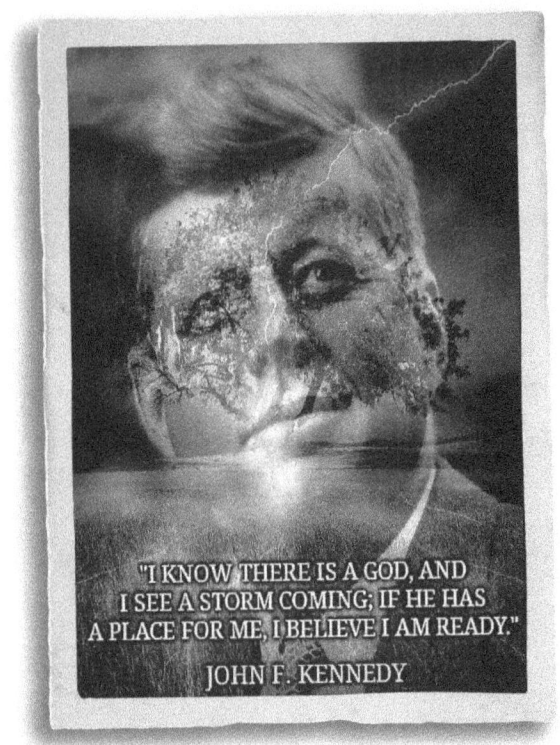

"I KNOW THERE IS A GOD, AND
I SEE A STORM COMING; IF HE HAS
A PLACE FOR ME, I BELIEVE I AM READY."

JOHN F. KENNEDY

As a little hand saluted a nation's sad voice,
This time in our history we will never rejoice.
His casket laid on a horse drawn wagon so bold
And the stars and stripes at half- mast unfold.

Questions of "why" in our hearts would burn
As our human spirits will somehow learn,
We will never know all the cruelties of mankind-
But forever a flame shall burn upon his shrine.

© November 22, 2003

In Honor of
JOHN FITZGERALD KENNEDY
Our 35th President

05/29/17-11/22/63

WHO IS MY MASTER?

Sacrifice my very soul, whatever it takes to win!

Gullible am I, the mortal thoughts from within;

Taken from me, I hate you!

Given to me, I love you,

Never enough it seems; a wicked world longs for you.

Cheat for me, buy for me,

Take me, for you own me.

The root of all evil, you shackle me like a dog's collar–

You almighty dollar!

© November 15, 2006

SLOW SIPS OF WINE

With your teasing laughter,
And slow sips of wine
Your eyes sparkle
As you pretend to be shy,
And you have that smile
That highlights your dimples.

Blue embroiders your blouse,
And your earrings glow,
But it's the passion in your eyes
I see…
And the heart I crave to know
Beneath the curves of your
Breasts…

© February 13, 2015

CLOUDS OF TIME

PAGES OF TIME

As we look at life with each turning of a page,
We smile and think of things that come of age,
Always working in our mind with things to do
Giving little thought of others point of view.

Voices crying out for peace and brotherhood,
With hope in this world of doing ourselves good.
Lives passing by like a flash from a lightning rod,
And we thought we could do it all without God.

Hidden deep within our spirit lays an endless quest,
To gain and accomplish without stopping to rest,
But our goals are filled with human discontent,
As though success was given its own sacrament.

We strive with little thought of today's good deed,
And leave our brother's to deal with their own need.
Draining life like water from the earth's crust,
Then we reach out to others with a hand of trust.

Should we've look at life from our humble knees,
And given an example that others could see–
Could we do better in the realms of a quiet mind,
And turned with care the "pages of time?"

© February 2001

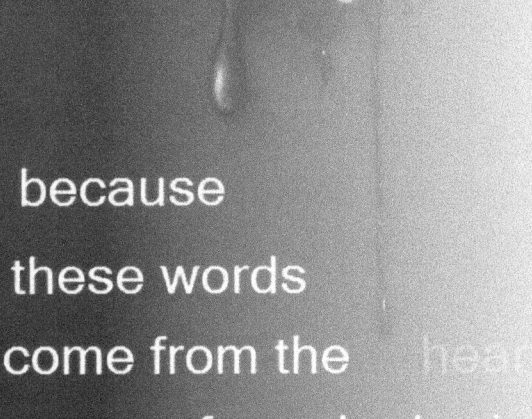

Listen to what people say when they cry

because these words come from the heart not from the brain

PERHAPS

Just thought you should know: I still love you!

The years have gone without a word spoken.

But time has not erased my thoughts of you,

So I guess your love for me was just a mere token

Of a time lost, or moments of forgotten feelings,

And now in my need I rush to tell you without delay,

That I was wrong for all of my deceitful dealings–

My hope is that I can somehow find a gentle way

To express words that has been locked behind a door

That may never be opened again, and I'm afraid

Of rejection, for this heart longs for something more,

Something to give back for the mistakes I've made.

Someday, perhaps, you will find a way to forgive me,

If only for a moment, this broken heart you'd see.

© January 3, 2007

LISTEN UP!

DEAR, let me whisper in your ear;
When we are in bed all alone,
Let your eyes never shed a tear
As I listen to you moan,
And your well will be filled up
In the throes of night:
So come and drink from loves cup!
As we wait for daylight.

It's all about passion, so I thought;

Moon shadows cast where you lay

In the moments of pleasure sought,

Cheers to the love you gave,

And to passion I'll never give up

Because it feels so right:

So come and drink from loves cup!

Love me with all of your might.

Listen up! Love is but a quest…

Its 4am says the hands on the clock,

And after love, there comes rest

Because upon my heart love knocked,

And when morning comes I'll get up

Then in your heart you will know:

What it's like to drink from loves cup!

And on your face it will show.

© September 24, 2018

PATCHWORK QUILT

From rags they were cut with hands of love,

Never the same size or color would they be,

But placed gently as though with a silk glove,

Then arrange patiently in a pattern with delicacy.

Endless hours were spent by the old wood heater,

Each stitch pulled to its perfect form and style,

Many have tried, but no one could beat her.

With a needle and thimble she sewed many a mile,

Here is the true meaning of her love given away,

Where the heart sings of joy and will never wilt!

By doing something for her family that will stay

As long as the old wooden frame didn't fall or tilt,

The colors of the rainbow would unfold each day

As winters faded under Mama's patchwork quilt.

© October 28, 2001

MY SOUL CRIES FOR YOU

What is wrong gentle soul?
For your tears I cannot hide,
This hurt inside you surely know,
Will these feelings ever subside?

Look into my eyes and see all this pain,
The sadness I hold from your absence.
Tell me darling our love was not in vain,
And free my spirit from all this nonsense.

When in my arms your warm touch I adore!
Now are only distant shadows in the night–
This love I feel for you will be forevermore,
And sadden for not being able to get it right.

I awake in the morning hour with wet eyes,
And wonder why you were in my dreams again?
Somewhere within this heart lie subtle cries,
Without understanding of how a love can end.

When loneliness sweetheart shrouds your mind,
Know that you once held a love that was true–
There will never be another so gentle and kind,
Could this be why "my soul cries for you?"

© March '2001

IN SILENCE I WEEP

Dear heart
This longing I have for you
The loneliness, the loneliness,
That grips my soul…
In silence I weep,
But I know tomorrow will come,
And you are not here!

Is it fair to say?
"That I miss you more than life!"
No I cannot undo yesterday,
And yes I was wrong…
In silence I weep,
But all I know is you are gone,
And I'm here all alone!

© February 5, 2024

KILLING TIME

I sat on the edge of the bed

With thoughts racing in my head

Again,

Will this be the last dream I have of her?

Shadows dancing

Around the bed, killing time

Is what I dread

There is nothing worse for me

Then to wonder, what is it that she wants

And why is it me

The night fades away, and stillness remains

Here in the darkness of time

Haunted by a dream

Of yesterday gone by

Where a love was lost

And now time

Is killing me

© August 21, 2012

You are my Beacon of Light... my Hope!
You are the Rock on which I stand!
You are the God in whom I trust,
The Alpha, the Omega, the First, the Last!
You are my Love...

And You are Love Everlasting!

A ROAD UNKNOWN

Into the darkness of life we drive
Not knowing our purpose or need,
And our freedom we take for granted,
Shackled by the lush of greed!

And I guess we think we'll live forever,
Then our focus turns to power—
And the need to self-indulge our soul,
Just to say, this is our finest hour!

I assure you history will repeat itself—
They said that Rome would never fall!
Yet it crumbled from the inside out!
While China survived behind its wall.

America, it's not a road unknown—
The influx of people we can't condone!

© April 2, 2018

39

COLORS OF MY SOUL

I wonder what lies beyond the next hill,
And the thought of this gives me a thrill!
I stare at the sea, and I wait upon the tide,
But the worst in me has to be my pride!
I look at a rose, and the thorns on its stem,
I wonder about hearts so many condemned—
The loss of love, and why a soul must mourn,
And where it once lived, secure and warm—
I look at the empty bed where we once slept,
And I think of all the promises not kept:
"I look at a mighty oak and all her leaves,
And I know in life it's only God I can please—
I think of the past, and all my eyes have seen,
And why are people so cruel and mean?"

© February 1, 2022

DID I FORGET

In a rhyme, isn't it a matter of time?
That the words of love are thrown
With great expectations of my mind!
Looking perfectly like a lovers' clone.

From one before me should I borrow?
Learning from things they did wrong!
Like a life lived with hurts and sorrow
In a heart where pain doesn't belong;

Did I forget, wasn't it a matter of time?
When life's storms decent from above;
Did it truly matter if my words rhyme?
Or isn't it just sweet words of love.

© February 7, 2015

HOLD ME WHILE I CRY

Why, could it just be the falling rain?
Or is it this loneliness driving me insane!
Could it be that my world is coming apart,
And there is no one here to comfort my heart.
Lord it's got to be the rain I need to blame…
When there was love I never had to complain;
Stop! This pain, brings out all the fears in me,
And a heart in despair needs love so desperately.
I guess I'm just feeling sorry for myself today,
And in my heart I know tomorrow I'll be okay.
Remembering the times I felt safe from harm,
And upon the satin sheets secure in your arms—
But the rain brings sadness as if one could die,
And I just need you to hold me while I cry.

© June 5, 2012

IN THE WINK OF AN EYE

Does love live where willows sway?
Maybe beside a waterfall,
Upon a distant hill where it rains,
Or does it matter at all.

Does it hide near the mossy stone?
Hidden so we cannot see
The mist rising from within our soul,
And it will never let us be.

Does it reside in the winds of time?
That crosses an ominous sky,
Or in the clouds that drifts forever,
Then it's gone in the wink of an eye.

© April 7, 2002

43

BEDROOM EYES

"O fairest Lady, with your bedroom eyes"
"Tell me, things of your heart you hide?"
Your beauty, "Unlike any I've ever known,
But your passion will come to my demise."

Your face brings light to the darkest night,
The hardest of hearts can't endure your sight;
What beauty my eyes can stare upon
Like the splendor of roses in the morning light.

When the mountains rise to kiss the sky,
Your beauty gives light where meadows loom,
And the shadows of clouds unveil my day
That brings joy to a heart that wants to cry.

© July 27, 2008

IT AIN'T EASY

Life as I see it…
Each day brings hope,
Look at the sky – look at the clouds
So be humble, and not so proud
Dance when no one is looking.

Life as I see it…
Look at the stars at night,
I cannot start to count them all!
Do this when your back is against the wall
Then problems will take a back seat.

Life as I see it…
Do good deeds – have happy thoughts
Take control of your mind
Peace and contentment you can find
It ain't easy, but it's the only life we have.

© April 8, 2023

INTOXICATING

I love your smile, the gleam in your eyes,
Your face speaks a thousand expressions.

I drown in the pool of your being…
And I could stay submerged there forever.

The bounce of your hair is an endless lure,
That leaves an imprint upon my soul.

I find I cannot get enough of you,
The mere touch of your hand is electrifying.

When you're near it's like lightning strikes,
The world disappears into total essence
As through the storms of life have gone forever.

Your voice is the sound of the morning dew,
And like the wind drifting on the meadow.

Your lips are like the fruit upon the vine,
They are as honey dripping from the hive,
And I must admit I'm weak in my knees.

How can your lure be so intoxicating?
Could it be from the love I see in your eyes?

© March 29, 2011

TONIGHT IS THE NIGHT

Tonight is the night
When love comes by–
It has to be true,
But I don't know why?
I'll make things right
We'll love all night
Just wait and see!

Tonight is the night
Soft music I will play
A perfect setting
You'll want to stay,

I'll hold you tight
I'll make things right
Just you and me!

Tonight is the night
It's passion we'll share
I'll make things right
"I love you," I'll declare,
Time will stand still
To love I will yield
Just let it be!

© April 15, 2023

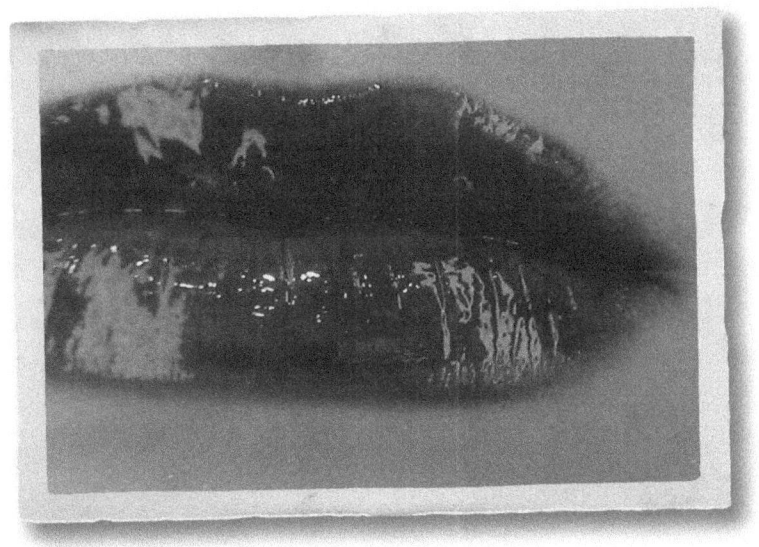

LIPS OF WINE

Kiss me with your lips of wine,
Leap into my arms from where you sit!
In time, your heart I shall find
With a passion your soul will not forget;
Be of good cheer, and never know sadness,
Say to me my kisses you have missed,
And here you will find no loneliness—
The taste of wine on your lips I've kissed.

© November 25, 2007

TENDER WAS THE NIGHT

We sat on the porch in the late afternoon as the sun went down
Sharing our thoughts of the day as we held each other close
Not blaming one another for what life has done to us—
Just accepting each other and being thankful for the moment.

In the back ground soft music is playing as we hum alone
Feelings of being lost and all alone are far from our minds—
It's like we have been here in this time and place in another life
Why is it that we feel we have known one another forever?

In the distance a train echo's sadness in the night air–

I notice there are moonbeams reflecting in your hair

As you turn to face me I can see the love in your eyes

I gently pull you close to me, and without words our lips meet.

My hand has gripped the back of your head – your back is arched

We are totally lost in the moment of inhibitions – breathless!

With these erotic needs that have long been buried deep within–

Now at last we can feel free to explore without judgment.

Our hearts are beating like ten thousand drums into the night

A passion has kindled that we thought was a long time dead

Now with these desires burning like embers in the fire–

The love we made and forever remember: "Tender was the Night."

© Oct '1999

IT ONLY HURTS A LITTLE WHILE

The sky is gray as the rain gently falls,
Blooms from a tree blows on the street,
The clouds above roll ever so quietly
Like the wind upon the fields of wheat.

And in a mulberry bush come sounds
Of birds building a nest as they sing,
Under the rose trellis Crocus blooms,
And the signs of summer are beginning.

I need you, love, I need you ever so near
As another season begins to retreat,
The rain starts to puddle on the ground
As the blooms wash across the street,

I need you more today than ever before
As this loneliness I can no longer hide,
And maybe your spirit can hear my cries
From this sadness that is locked inside.

Time drifts like the rain pouring outside,
For time is something I cannot hold

Like blooms from a tree they're soon gone,
But this love for you will never grow old.

It seems that life sets its own course
Upon the winds with their endless climb,
It brings the seasons without command,
But I know that I cannot conquer time.

The sky is now blue after the rain stops,
And my thoughts of you brings me a smile,
Maybe someday all of this pain will end…
Hoping it only hurts a little while.

© March 18, 2004

LEAVES OF AUTUMN

When autumn begins
It's like sweet violins,
And to my heart you sing!

O the sweet sound
As the wind plays around,
And autumn takes wing.

Shadows fall on shadows,

The corn is golden brown,

And sadness runs deep.

The birds fly over

The rabbits in the clover,

And summer will sleep.

And deep in my soul

Only God knows

Where Jack Frost hides;

Leaves of autumn–

It's like violins,

Then God decides

When winter begins.

© November 9, 2015

KISSED BY DESIRE

WISDOM OF ANTS

The people trample above me without any notice,
As though I have little or no meaning to their lives.
A few kneel to observe the knowledge that I impart,
But like the blowing winds, their minds are fleeting.

All things were placed upon this earth for a purpose,
But most people are too busy to grasp life's meaning!

And they forget that what they sow, they will also reap,
But when they are weak that is when they are strong.

The ground trembles beneath your hurried journey,
Without any thought of what your shadow has cast.
Planning for the future is your ultimate goal in life,
And today was only a blur that just got in your way.

Your ego seems to be your worst enemy on this path,
You cram your head with ideas and meaningless facts,
And you seek wisdom so you won't feel inadequate,
Then forgot to live today while grabbing for tomorrow.

Did you notice that it is in patience I securely wait?
Because God promises that spring will come in time.
Why do you seek the things of this life, which fades?
For you too will return to dust from whence you came.

Come and observe me; consider my ways and be wise!
For I have no commander, no overseer or ruler,
I store my provisions in summer, and gather at harvest,
For this wisdom shall preserve the life of its possessor.

© March 14, 2001

PRIDE GOTH

Life, a journey that will someday end,

And it matters what truth we hold inside.

We all start with good intentions, but then,

I have to ask, "Was it done for selfish pride?"

I am not here to make judgment on you,

But to help explain life's challenging game.

The pitfalls in life are always out of view,

With knowledge there is no one to blame!
Those before us put things in our head
That makes us want to pull out our hair!
I ask, "What was their purpose or agenda,"
You see, life at its best is not always fair!
Was it God's law or another's referenda?
Or just mere words that man has said.
Know that I'd like to lend a helping hand
Not to hurt you, but give insight instead;
The world is full of empty words spoken,
And the world will take advantage if it can!
Leaving you with heartaches as it's token.

Remember: "pride Goth before the fall,"
And there are stones that others will cast,
But listen, your enter spirit will always call,
And know that only God's wisdom will last!

© December 8, 2013

MORNING AFTER

I will not bathe myself this day;
The smell of you lingers, on me,
For you slept in my arms all night.

© January 3, 2011

THE DANCE

The smell of candles burning fills the air,
And the sweet taste of wine is on your lips.
The passion drips from your enchanting eyes,
As we sway across the floor in perfect form.
The music in our souls embraces this moment,
As though our hearts had never been apart.
In this forgotten time is what is real in life,
And the years have waited patiently for us–
Gracefully our feet float with gentle harmony,
Across the pages that were lost in yesterday–
To a place our enduring love shall never die,
And the sweet sounds of violins will surely play!
In a precious moment to love I make this stance:
Forever holding dear memories of "The Dance."

© June 1, 2001

WHERE HAS LOVE GONE

The sting of love
I remember the passion–
This heart pounds
Kisses forever so sweet!
Seduced by euphoria–
But why did we meet?

Fragments of a heart
Love held in my hands–

So tender are you,
That we once were
The essence of passion—
These thoughts of her.

The sting of love
I remember the passion—
My heart cries out
It hurts to the bone—
A broken man
Left all alone.

The sting of love
I remember the passion—
And I need you so,
But life must go on—
My bed is now empty
Where has love gone?

© July 26, 2020

TOO LATE TO CRY

Along the long roads of time,
I stop, I look, and I clear my mind–
A lot of questions, and I don't why,
But I guess time just goes on by.

I enjoy a glass of wine by candlelight,
It just seems to make the world right–
In the meadow the wind begins to lie,
But I guess time just goes on by!

The nights always brings a quiet hush,
When this old world is not in a rush—
After a bottle of wine I'm pretty high,
But I guess time just goes on by!

I think of life and where I've been,
And I wonder how it will all end—
Then I hang my head and want to cry,
But I guess time just goes on by!

We are all given the same time in a day,
And it's up to us how we choose to play—
There'll always be dark clouds in the sky,
But I guess time just goes on by!

Sometimes we win – sometimes we fail,
The water we drink is from our own well—
And this I can assure you, we all will die,
Then reality! "It will be too late to cry!"

© April 17, 2024

Listen to what people say
when they cry

because
these words
come from the heart
not from the brain

MY FIRST HEARTACHE

Since my first heartache
I have thought to myself,
"Why does love hurt?"
Like a thousand dreams
I have thought of you
You're perfect in form
Each part in place,
And your passion–
O your tender passion!

I am in awe with the thought of you,
And I dream of you in my arms until daybreak,
And now I ask, "why does love hurt?"
Why does my heart ache?

© August 17, 2016

KINDRED SPIRIT

My dearest love,

I don't know why I have this need to write this letter to you? Maybe it's because I have allowed the years to slowly slip away. I remember the first time I saw you. There you were in front of me, and I was overtaken by your beauty. Then totally out of character I wink at you – then unexpectedly you winked back. From that day forward I was never the same. There is no way I can put into words how I felt! This was truly the only time in my life that my heart ached for another.

I was one of those people that never believed in love at first sight. But with you I can now confess that it was love at first sight. I was smitten for life! At first I just played it off as an infatuation – there was no way I would allow anything or anyone to have control over me, even love! Damn!

"Those blue eyes looking back at me." How was I able to resist the way you looked at me? But as fate would have it there were circumstances that set the course of life.

It's been twenty years now since the last time I saw you. With that said, I guess that's why I'm writing this letter – you see love, there is some unfinished business between you and me! I know I did a few crazy things, and for that I owe you an apology. I suspect that you thought I was stalking you – well I can assure you that part is not true! Now I admit there were times I wanted to find you! I even sent a letter to what I thought was your address expressing my love for you, but I assume you never got it or you chose not to respond.

Love, have you ever heard the saying, "Looking for a needle in a haystack?"

Well those are the odds of you ever reading this letter. But what the hell – what do I have to lose? I can assure you that stranger things have happened. There are many roads in life, but true love only travels one.

So here I am on Bird Island, NC placing a letter in an old Mailbox that reads "Kindred Spirit." I'm laughing as I'm leaving this letter – reminds me that fools in love never learn! After all these years my love – I'm still in love with you, and if fate is kind hopefully we will meet again.

© November 14, 2020

LADIES OF THE NIGHT

The three ladies sat under a tree,
They were as naked as they could be.

One of them said to her mate,
'Where shall we our victims take?'

Lure him to the river or a dusty field,
There we lay him down at his own will.

'His clothes will fall around his feet,
Tonight he sells his soul too cheap.'

'His weaknesses they take so eagerly,
Without any thought of guilt to be.'

Lures of the night brings no regret,
But tomorrow has not come yet.

They toy with thoughts in his head,
As though his emotions were dead.

They lie upon their naked backs,
Like warm bread before it cracks.
They steal his spirit before his prime,
And these memories stay a long time.

Ladies of the night wait with a plan,
To pray on the weaknesses of a man.

© July 13, 2006

BEHIND THE SHOJI SCREEN

The mornings are so precious to me,
For the night brought thoughts of you,
These little treasures of your spirit,
Hidden in my memory just out of view.

Deep in the shadows of this mind,
Where love is stored for no one to see,

Lies a sad heart because of your absence,
And I wonder if time will set me free?

If I should put you in a strong box,
Then take you out from time to time
To polish you like a precious jewel,
Would this keep you always in mind?

I shall always carry you in my heart,
And I promised myself never to forget
How your beauty reflect life's meaning,
In my darkest world, but yet,

I still feel that true love conquers all,
And without it you're surely deprived
Because if you settle for anything less,
Then you're no longer alive.

So as my tears fall upon my pillow,
As I lie down to sleep I shall dream,
That you will find my spirit once again,
Waiting here behind the Shoji screen.

© November 17, 2001

I'VE CRIED ENOUGH

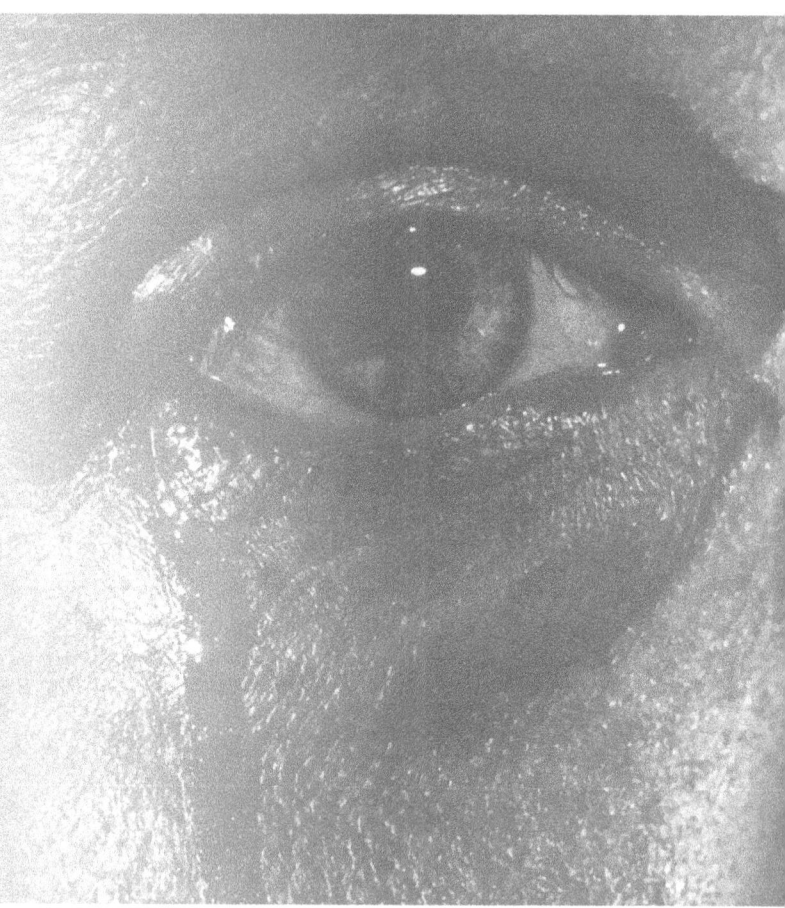

Hurt, pain, sadness as tears come with ease
A love I can't please
The heart is always battling with the mind
Like war and peace that can't be defined.

When love is in bloom the heart will say:
"Let passion shine, and never fade away."

Truth has to be revealed, this is a must
It's like a friend that you will always trust.

Love is like the wind that comes in haste,
Or like the sweetness of honey we taste.

When love is right, you need not to compare
It's like fingers in your hair;
Love has to be refined like a rare piece of art,
And when it comes to you let it fill your heart.

© March 25, 2012

A METAPHOR

While walking by the sea…
A thought that came to me:
Have I ever been here before?

I listen to the waves as they cap…
In my mind are memories that overlap:
Her love I don't have anymore!

When the days are hot and long…
The seagulls no longer have a song:
The tide will have no shore.

Then in my heart – I need to cry…
As the dark clouds pass on by:
These feelings I cannot ignore!

I walked slowly by the sea (a metaphor)
But her love I'll need forevermore!

© *April 20, 2023*

REAP WHAT WE SOW

I have decided to tune out the world,
It's time to turn the tide–
There is nothing that I can do anyway
What matters is how I feel inside!

Everywhere I turn its endless madness,
And it's heartache and pain–
I'm telling you – Satan is alive and well,
And to partake in this is insane!

I have decided to tune out the world,
And focus on what is good–
Just notice the beauty of a sunrise…
The meaning of life is understood!

"Be still and know that I am God!
You spoiled the child by sparing the rod!"

© June 7, 2024

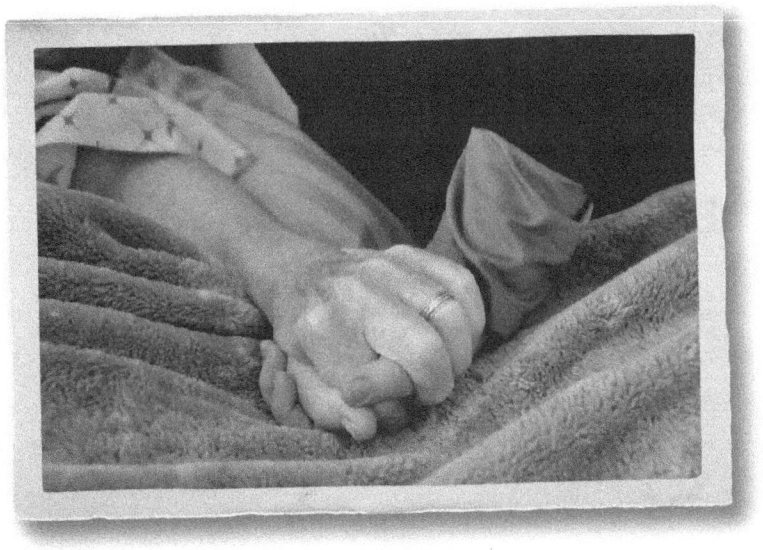

THE AGE OF WISDOM

Of yesterdays', the saddest of all
Is when a precious love dies!
The tears that rushes to our eyes:
Brings a heartache beyond reprise,
And in this moment we must realize
Life, in short, has no compromise.
Of yesterdays', not forgotten I recall,
When a soul departs from this life
It matters not if they toiled with strife;
The journey made to their afterlife,
And now this grief cuts like a knife!
The age of wisdom: Live and love,
And know that this life is so finite–
For each moment comes from above.

© December 13, 2015

POOLS OF BLUE

Thy heart searches for thee.
Eyes, like pools of blue, see me!
Thy heart ponders why.
Needing your touch, the tears I cry.

I stand in the summer showers,
And seek your image for hours.
Oh! Pools of blue, I long for thee,
To see this love that lies in me.

© March 31, 2005

MIDNIGHT SONATA

Autumn filled evening

Chilled champagne

Erotic candles gleam

Perfume intoxicating

Eyes registered in awe

Hearts pounding

Lips wet with wine

Anticipation

Enraptured by allure

Embraced in arms

Luscious taste of love

Entangled passion

Fingers enmeshed in hair

Clothes falling

Satin sheets lingering

Burning desires

Tracing bodies

Totally uninhibited

Muscles tighten

Breathless

Screaming

Unleashed emotions

Gasping for truth

Luminous colors

Tears of triumph

Sweet whispers

Closeness

Drifting silence

Sensual panacea for

Tranquility

Adorned with

Gentle echoes of the

Midnight sonata.

© November, 2000

WHEN YOU KISS ME

Sweet kisses, I never regret,

To love there is never an end;

The love you give – is the love you get,

But you have to let love in:

Troubles in life – they make me sad,

And I ask, "How can this be?"

And my heart breaks, but may I add,

Life is better when you kiss me!

© January 4, 2018

AT JOURNEY'S END

The heavens smiled when you were born,
Oh! The hearts you would touch along the way.
Church bells rang out while the angels adorned
Mountaintops that would reflect upon your day.
The love you gave to others is without compare,
And your heart was as tender as a blissful dove.
A gentle touch from your hands was with care,
And it all was given with unconditional love.

Heaven holds a special place for people like you,

That gave without any thoughts of personal gain;

When you were around the sky was always blue,

And the dark clouds of this life shed no rain.

So when the angels came to take you home,

There is a sadness that we have never known,

But in our sadness a quiet voice whispers:

"You will go out in joy

and be led forth in peace;

the mountains and hills

will burst into song before you,

and all the trees of the field

will clap their hands."

For it is not in this life where you have been,

But it's where you're going at journey's end.

© July 24, 2004

INNOCENCE OF THE DAY

It was a late afternoon as I walk alone kicking a can
Not yet understanding the perils of being a man
The winds of life now seem more than a lad of ten can bear
Feelings of anger, confusion, and who if any will care.

Sitting in this apple tree with my salt shaker in hand
Remembering the gentle voice saying son lets work the land
Being in church on Sunday morning was Dad's golden rule
As we made our way to our favorite pew.

Kneeling by the bedside to pray; the words that he would say:

"Lord I lay me down to sleep my soul is yours to keep

Knowing what we sow in this life we shall also reap

Teach me your wisdom O Lord for we are only your sheep."

They say there is nothing under the sun that's going to last

But why was I forced to grow up so fast?

It seems like only yesterday when Dad and I would run and play

Now I just seem lost holding all this hurt – words I cannot say.

It was a winter's day as we tracked the rabbits through the snow

Stepping in his footprints he turns to let me know:

"Son you know that means you will never tell your Dad a lie!"

But how could one so young imagine that he would soon die?

Without the hand of guidance life will come and go as it may

What we learn when we are young will keep us until our dying day

This journey of my life has not always been easy for this I can say:

It is only now that I can understand the "Innocence of the day."

© September 1999

IF THESE WALLS COULD TALK

Yesterday, when we stood by the old mill
I saw your love meant for only me,
And nothing is as dearest to me still,
The moments in life I still hold for thee,

But it seems that yesterday was my demise,
This heartache that remains in me,
Darling, how I remember those pretty eyes,
And now your memory won't let me be!

If these walls could only talk…
Only God knows what they would say:
Yesterday my love, life's little short walk,
For a heart of love, and a heart of play.

Epaphroditus© December 5, 2015

KISS ME LIKE YOU MEAN IT!

A man I am, yet I can think

And from your cup I will drink;

It is your passion I shall partake,

I will pursue you, make no mistake!

It is your spirit that gives me delight,

Kiss me like you mean it, don't fight!

Fill thy cup; let it flow like a flood

Chilling your spine, boiling your blood;

A man I am, and therefore I say:

"Kiss me! Drink of passion, and let's play."

© January 11, 2011